TEXT AND PHOTOGRAPHY BY Susan Hazen-Hammond

THUNDER BEAR

and

KO

The Buffalo Nation and Nambe Pueblo

DUTTON CHILDREN'S BOOKS   NEW YORK

This book is dedicated to the memory of Donna Riley, artist and storyteller.

Deepest thanks to the people of Nambe Pueblo, particularly Herbert Yates, Ben Yates, Thunder Bear Yates, Shannon McKenna, Karen Denilaikai, Denise Perez, Lela Kaskalla, Victor Lujan, Cloud Eagle, and Gary Montowine.

Special thanks to Susan Arritt, Don MacCarter, and Elizabeth King, who started me on the path toward this book.

Thanks to photographers Sam Abell, Eduardo Fuss, Charles Mann, Christine Preston, Michael DiBari, and Judy Gordon for their insight and support. Thanks also to Pat Martin, Wendy McEahern, and the staff at Visions Photo Lab.

Thanks to Angela and Karl Storch, Elena and Flavio Garcia, Schia Muterperl, Iska Sargent, Peggy van Hulsteyn, Fred and Jann Kline, Margret Henkels, William and Beth Hammond, and the members of No Poets and Writers at Elaine's for their nurturing support. And a special thanks to Ken Duerre, Paul Golding, and Ken Macrorie for their support and encouragement as I worked on this book.

Above all, thanks to my editor, Susan Van Metre, and designer, Amy Berniker, without whom this book could not have come into existence.

PRONUNCIATION GUIDE

Apache (uh-PATCH-ee)
chicharras (chee-CHAR-ras)
Choctaw (CHAHK-tah)
Jemez (HEH-mehz)
Keresan (kuh-REE-zun)
kiva (KEE-vah)
ko (koh)
mano (MAH-no)
metate (meh-TAH-tay)
Nambe Pueblo (nahm-BAY PWE-bloh)
Navajo (NAH-vah-ho)
Picuris (pick-oo-REES)
piñon (pin-YOHN)
Pojoaque (poh-HWAH-kay)
San Ildefonso (sahn ill-duh-FAWN-so)
San Juan (sahn HWAN)
Taos (TAH-ohs)
Tewa (TAY-wah)
Tiwa (TEE-wah)
Towa (TOW-wah)
Zuni (ZOO-nee)

Text and photography copyright © 1999 by Susan Hazen-Hammond
All rights reserved.

CIP Data is available.
Published in the United States 1999 by Dutton Children's Books,
a division of Penguin Putnam Books for Young Readers
345 Hudson Street, New York, New York 10014
http://www.penguinputnam.com/yreaders/index.htm

Designed by Amy Berniker
Printed in Hong Kong
First Edition
10 9 8 7 6 5 4 3 2 1
ISBN 0-525-46013-6

As far back as Thunder Bear Yates can remember, there have always been buffalo at Nambe Pueblo. His father, Ben, is the tribe's Buffalo Keeper. And Thunder Bear has always liked to go with him to the 180-acre buffalo range and look after the herd.

But Thunder Bear knows that back in the days before his memory began, no buffalo roamed the wrinkled hills of his northern New Mexico homeland. Long ago, on the nearby plains, non-Indian hunters killed so many that the animals became nearly extinct, and Thunder Bear's ancestors lost both a source of food and a spiritual brother. It was Thunder Bear's family who helped bring the buffalo back into the life of the Pueblo.

Like most of us, eight-year-old Thunder Bear has a little of this and a little of that in him, a little Scottish and a little Choctaw Indian. But mostly, he is a Pueblo Indian, a member of one of nineteen Pueblo tribes that have lived in New Mexico for over a thousand years.

The Pueblo peoples of New Mexico are divided into five groups, speaking five languages—Tewa, Towa, Tiwa, Keresan, and Zuni.

The word *pueblo* means "village" in Spanish. In the 1500s, Spanish explorers gave the Pueblo peoples this name because, instead of living in tents or other temporary homes, they lived year-round in compact, permanent villages made of stone or hardened mud.

Pueblo villages have always been small. Nambe Pueblo probably never held more than a thousand residents. Today it looks more like a scattering of houses spread across the countryside than a town.

At first glimpse, Nambe Pueblo could be any community in northern New Mexico. Many houses have flat roofs, and the smooth plaster on the walls conceals the mud bricks, called adobes.

Even Thunder Bear's house looks like any ordinary home in northern New Mexico, except that his father has painted bear tracks, kiva steps, and thunderclouds on the wall that faces the setting sun. These symbols remind visitors that bears, rain, and all of nature are sacred to the Pueblo Indians. The kiva steps symbolize the kiva, the sacred ceremonial chamber.

Kivas have always been the most important structures in any Pueblo village. You might say that to the Pueblo Indians, the kiva is a little like a church, although it's not that simple. For many, every act of ordinary life—even riding the bus to school—has a spiritual meaning. Worship isn't done in just one special place.

Long ago, kivas were mainly for men and boys. Boys left their mothers and sisters and went to live in the kiva when they were about seven. There the wise old men of the tribe passed on to them the sacred teachings and history of the ancestors. It was a little like going to school, but there was no reading or writing. Young people learned by listening to and working with their elders.

Thunder Bear's ancestors also performed ceremonies in the kiva. In the summer, they honored the corn and the rituals of planting and harvesting. In the winter, they honored animals and the spirits of the animals that fed the people.

Today, both men and women can enter the kiva, and boys no longer go there to live, but the kiva is still a sacred place where rituals are performed that no outsider can witness. The kiva is a reminder to Pueblo peoples of the traditions that set them apart from the Hispanics, Anglos, Apaches, Navajos, and other ethnic groups that also live in northern New Mexico.

In some ways, Thunder Bear is just an ordinary American kid. When he is not in school, he likes to toss baseballs up in the air and catch them in his mitt. He likes to go fishing and clean his own fish. He likes to poke at campfires with a stick. He likes to watch the water at Nambe Falls splashing down across the black rocks.

But Thunder Bear never forgets that he is also a Pueblo Indian. Like his ancestors before him, he greets the morning sun with sacred cornmeal, and he offers the first bites of every meal to the spirits that dwell in each of the four sacred directions—north, east, south, and west.

In Thunder Bear's living room, buffalo headdresses sit on the coffee table next to his father's cell phone. In the dining room, skins of deer, antelope, and other animals his father has hunted hang over the curtain rod. Below them sits the computer where Thunder Bear does his homework.

In the freezer, Thunder Bear's father keeps a bag of baked *chicharras*, insects that people in other places call cicadas. After his father soaks the *chicharras* in brine and roasts them in a hot oven for an hour, they taste pretty good, sort of like potato chips. Sometimes, while Thunder Bear and Ben are munching *chicharras*, his father talks about the ancestors and why the buffalo were so important to them.

In ancient times, during the spring, summer, and fall, the people worked in their fields, growing corn, beans, and squash. In the winter they hunted for their food.

At least once each winter, the ancestors would travel east for several days, to the plains of eastern New Mexico. There they would hunt *ko. Ko* is the name for buffalo in Tewa, the language of Thunder Bear's ancestors.

Today, the people of Nambe still follow an ancient tradition in which some families belong to the Winter People and others to the Summer People. Long ago, every act of daily life was accompanied by a prayer, a thought, or a song. Summer People were in charge of the rituals of summer, related to planting and harvesting corn and other crops. Winter People were responsible for honoring animals and the hunt for large game, such as buffalo. The Pueblo peoples believed that a buffalo cow was the symbolic mother of all large game animals. Today, buffalo have a special importance to the Pueblo, and particularly to Winter People like Thunder Bear.

Maybe that is why, after school, Thunder Bear likes to watch the buffalo calves drink milk by nursing from their mother's udders. In the late-afternoon light, a calf's coat glows bright orange against its mother's dark brown hair. The buffalo seem at peace, as if they and the people of the Pueblo had never been parted.

It was Thunder Bear's grandfather, Herbert Yates, who helped bring the buffalo back to Nambe Pueblo.

Decades ago, the old ways were in danger of dying out at Nambe. So the religious leaders at the nearby Pueblo of San Ildefonso chose Herbert Yates to become the spiritual leader of the Winter People at Nambe Pueblo.

In ancient times, it would have meant that, every year during the cold season, he was the ruler of the entire village. Today, it means that Herbert Yates is the spiritual father of the Winter People and, by extension, of all six hundred inhabitants of Nambe Pueblo. He helps them stay connected to the traditions and beliefs of the past.

Herbert has selected his son Ben to become the leader of the Winter People after him. And Ben has decided that someday, when Thunder Bear is a grown man, he will become the leader of the Winter People of Nambe Pueblo.

When Herbert was trying to think of ways to interest his people in the past, he decided that the Pueblo needed more physical reminders of the old times, so—with the approval of the people of the Pueblo—he created a buffalo herd. Since buffalo no longer lived on the plains of eastern New Mexico, Herbert brought animals from faraway places like Montana and the Dakotas. They became Nambe Pueblo's first buffalo herd. Ben became the first Buffalo Keeper.

So Thunder Bear grew up with buffalo, and as a young child he didn't think much about their spiritual importance. In fact, he had trouble concentrating on all of the Pueblo beliefs—it seemed as if there was so much to learn. He felt overwhelmed. Thunder Bear liked the buffalo, but they just seemed like animals to him.

Then one day, when he was seven, he overheard his father and his grandfather discussing a place called Fort Wingate.

"There's nothing wrong with the state owning buffalo if they want," his grandfather was saying. "But we have always honored the buffalo. We would never kill a buffalo just for the fun of it."

The words made Thunder Bear anxious. He thought of their buffalo herd, and a sick feeling hit his stomach as he imagined people shooting them just to have a good time.

Later Ben told Thunder Bear that the State of New Mexico owned a herd of about seventy buffalo, which was kept at a former Army fort called Wingate, about two hundred miles west. For thirty years the buffalo had lived there peacefully, protected from hunters. But now the state had decided to allow hunters to kill some of the animals.

Picuris Pueblo, north of Nambe, and a group of buffalo-owning tribes called the Inter-tribal Bison Cooperative had joined a lawsuit to stop the hunt. Ben read Thunder Bear the words. They sounded stiff. "'Plaintiffs have environmental, esthetic, cultural, and spiritual interests in protecting the bison from sport hunting.'"

"What does that mean?" Thunder Bear asked.

"Thousands of years ago, buffalo roamed across the whole continent," Ben explained. "That was the beginning of the buffalo nation. Ever since then, buffalo have been our brothers. Indians have never hunted for the fun of it; even today we hunt only for food. It's not good, this business of allowing buffalo to be hunted for sport. The buffalo are sacred."

In the old days, before Europeans arrived, Indians hunted with spears or with bows and arrows. The buffalo had a chance. But, according to the legal documents, hunting a buffalo with a gun was like shooting a parked car.

After that, Thunder Bear paid more attention to the buffalo that already lived at Nambe Pueblo. He noticed how, as a calf grew older, its orange hair gradually turned brown. He saw adult buffalo lock horns and butt their heads together when one got in the other's way. He listened to them grunt, and he watched how they used their tongues to keep their nostrils moist. His dad explained that buffalos' nostrils are made of delicate skin, something like the skin on the inside of a human being's lips. If buffalo didn't keep their nostrils moist, they might dry out, crack, and become infected. Ordinary farm cattle keep their nostrils wet, too.

Thunder Bear noticed that the buffalo seemed to know that the people of Nambe would treat them well. During times when there wasn't enough wild grass to fill their stomachs, the animals would walk right up to the back of Ben's truck to eat hay.

Once, when Ben brought a visitor into the buffalo range, she fed a buffalo hay from her hands. But Ben cautioned her that in other places, where buffalo don't feel so safe, it would be dangerous to get so close. Even at Nambe Pueblo, it wouldn't be safe for an outsider to approach a buffalo if Ben weren't around.

As Thunder Bear accompanied his father on his trips to the buffalo range, he noticed that normally, when a buffalo has an itch, it uses a hoof or leg to scratch itself. But in the spring, when the animals' heavy winter coat falls out in clumps, they itch all over and look for things to rub against.

Sometimes when the buffalo are molting, they rub against one of the stubby piñon or juniper trees scattered across the landscape. Long strands of woolly hair come off and cling to the needles like the fleece of a brown sheep.

One day an enormous buffalo bull used the hood of a visiting photographer's car to scratch the underside of his neck.

His head was so big it reached all the way from the bumper to the windshield.

"Go away," the photographer shouted. But the buffalo ignored her until he had finished scratching.

After that, her car had a loose bumper and a dimple in the hood. But she was lucky it wasn't worse. The shaggy animals have enormous strength, and a single buffalo can weigh 2,500 pounds, ten times as much as a pro football player. Of course, to the photographer, who was worried about her car, it looked as if the buffalo weighed much more than that.

From his father, Thunder Bear learned that even though most people use the word *buffalo*, scientists call the animals bison. Once, sixty million buffalo roamed across all of North America, though climate changes eventually limited them mainly to the Great Plains.

The buffalo were important to the early Pueblo people. Every part of the animal had a use. Hides became robes, and they could be used like money to buy food or other items. Buffalo bones became tools. Hollow horns became drinking cups. Tribes in other parts of the continent turned the hides into one-person boats, shaped like tubs, which were light enough to be carried piggyback to water. Some of these tribes also burned buffalo dung when firewood ran out.

In all the time buffalo were hunted by Indians, there was never any danger that they would become extinct—not until non-Indians came along. During the 1870s alone, non-Indian hunters killed more than a million buffalo a year. By the 1890s, only 1,500 buffalo remained.

"It must have been a terrible loss to our ancestors when *ko* was gone," Ben told Thunder Bear. "Even though they were farmers, they depended on *ko* for so much. But now *ko* is coming back."

Today more than 75,000 buffalo live in the United States and Canada. Some live on Indian reservations across the West, among people who have honored them for thousands of years.

Others live on private land belonging to non-Indian ranchers. Some live on government land, like Fort Wingate.

It seemed to Thunder Bear as if the adults were talking about the buffalo at Fort Wingate almost every day. Several Pueblos, including Nambe, San Juan, Taos, Picuris, and Pojoaque, were trying to convince the state to turn some buffalo over to them.

People from the Pueblos talked to state legislators. They talked to the New Mexico Department of Game and Fish. They talked to reporters. But mostly they talked to one another.

"The Indian nation and the buffalo nation have been linked since time began," Ben told Thunder Bear. "If we can save the buffalo, we will be saving ourselves."

One day, his father told his grandfather in discouragement, "I'm afraid there's no hope. The hunt is going to happen. And the worst of it is, there will be no one there to bless the buffalo when they die—no one there to carry out the sacred rituals."

According to Pueblo beliefs, when a buffalo dies, those present must sprinkle sacred cornmeal on its head. Four days later, they bury the jawbone at a secret ceremonial site so that the spirit of the animal can return to the earth and be reborn. In this way, there will always be enough animals to hunt. In this way, no hunter will ever forget the sacredness of the animal whose life he is taking.

For months, Thunder Bear's father and grandfather hardly smiled. Thunder Bear knew that the problem with the buffalo at Fort Wingate was nothing like the problems his ancestors or the ancestors of the buffalo had faced. But sometimes it felt as if there wasn't much point in honoring ancient customs if nothing could be done to keep outsiders from killing the buffalo.

Like his father and his grandfather, Thunder Bear grew quiet.

But finally good news came. A federal judge called off the hunt. The state agreed to turn over twenty-five buffalo from Fort Wingate to the Pueblo tribes. Five animals would go to Nambe Pueblo. The buffalo that remained at Fort Wingate would be safe.

In private ceremonies, Thunder Bear's grandfather and other villagers prepared themselves spiritually for the arrival of the buffalo.

One cold morning in February, while Herbert stayed behind in the village and Thunder Bear went off to school at Pojoaque Pueblo, Ben and men from the other villages drove to Fort Wingate. There a helicopter herded the animals, a few at a time, into a corral. The animals weren't used to being penned up or being around people. They thought they were going to die. They stormed back and forth.

As they worked, Ben and the other men spoke quietly to the buffalo in Tewa or in Tiwa, the language of Picuris and Taos Pueblos. But once, a buffalo bull lowered his head and pawed the frozen ground, preparing to charge Ben. Ben swung himself up on the fence. Then he reentered the pen, trying to calm the animals with his presence.

Gradually the buffalo quieted down and were moved one by one into a handling cage. Then Ben, who knew buffalo better than anyone else, helped the veterinarian put identification tags in their ears and vaccinate them. This frightened the buffalo again, making it tricky to release them back into the pen. The two men almost got trampled.

Meanwhile, back at Nambe Pueblo, people were getting excited about the arrival of the buffalo. Many who worked away from the Pueblo during the week were glad that the buffalo would come on a Saturday, when they could be there to greet them.

Thunder Bear was excited, too. He and three other children from the Pueblo were going to perform the buffalo dance.

That Saturday, a cold, gray day, someone put up a sign at the buffalo range that said: BUFFALO ARRIVE AT 3:00.

The villagers waited. At about 4:30, the truck carrying the buffalo for Nambe, San Juan, and Taos Pueblos came into view. People filled their hands with sacred cornmeal. Before they sprinkled it through the slats of the truck onto the buffalo, Herbert Yates told the photographers that this ritual was like the rituals in the kiva: too sacred to be photographed.

"It is not the Pueblo way," he said.

Then he offered a prayer in Tewa to the buffalo and the spirits of all buffalo that have ever lived.

The men let the buffalo themselves choose which ones stayed at Nambe. When the back of the truck opened, five buffalo sprang out, one at a time.

The shaggy animals rushed to the far fence, where the other buffalo greeted them. For a long time, the new herd walked side by side with the old, with only a fence between them.

Thunder Bear watched. He and the other young dancers were wearing traditional costumes, made by family members and passed down from generation to generation.

Each part of the costume has a meaning. Because skunks stink, the skunk fur around the ankles protects from evil. The turquoise symbolizes winter. The gourd rattles imitate the sound of falling rain, and the feathers stand for the sky. The fur headdresses represent the buffalo.

The wind was cold as Thunder Bear and the other children began to move their feet up and down, back and forth, in the same ancient rhythm that their ancestors used. But they didn't feel the cold. It seemed as if their feet had always known these steps.

With each movement, Thunder Bear and the other dancers honored the spirits of the buffalo—those that had come to Nambe and those that had stayed behind at Fort Wingate, as well as all the buffalo that had lived and died since time began.

As Thunder Bear rattled his gourd and felt the weight of the buffalo headdress on his head, a sense of strength surged through him. The buffalo nation had survived against terrible odds. It seemed to him as if the animals were sharing their power with him.

When Thunder Bear finished dancing, he and another buffalo dancer locked their horns like real buffalo bulls. Thunder Bear could almost feel what it was like to be a buffalo. And he could almost feel what it was going to be like to be the leader of the Winter People.

For the first time in his life, Thunder Bear knew, without a single doubt, that he was up to the challenges of learning to be the leader of the Winter People. He knew he wasn't wise now, but someday he would be—wise like his father, wise like his grandfather, wise like his ancestors.

Even though Thunder Bear said nothing, his grandfather seemed to understand how he felt. He said, "Giving these animals a home will be a kind of renewal. The buffalo will remind us of our traditions. They'll help us get back in touch with who we really are, as Native Americans, as the people of Nambe Pueblo."

It was true. That summer, for the first time, the village hosted a camp to teach Native American traditions. Even Thunder Bear's baby sister, Tewa Breeze, arrived one evening in the arms of their teen-aged half sister. The little girl wore a traditional costume.

That night, just before dark, Thunder Bear's grandfather came to the evening campfire gathering and spoke.

"Each winter before our ancestors went hunting, they prayed first to the spirits of the animals," he said. "They believed the animals talked among themselves and decided which one would sacrifice itself so that people would have food and could survive." After a hunter killed an animal, he thanked it for providing food for his family and friends.

At the summer camp, the young people practiced shooting bows and arrows. Thunder Bear loved to pull the bow back and send the arrow zinging through the air. It flew so fast that it made a humming sound.

Ben taught the young people how to make their own bows and arrows. For arrows, he cut straight sticks from a bush called Apache plume. Then he scraped the wood with a knife to make it smooth. The bows were made from strong oak branches, stripped of their bark and bent into shape.

Early one evening, Ben took Thunder Bear and his younger brother, Aaron, out into the countryside. When the last light glowed above the Jemez Mountains in the west, the three sat on the ground and made arrows. As Thunder Bear sat there, scraping the wood with a knife, he thought to himself that none of this would have happened if it hadn't been for the buffalo. Or maybe it would have happened, but he wouldn't have appreciated it the way he appreciated it now.

Now he understood that everything he was doing was preparing him to become the leader of the Winter People. Much of what he was learning had nothing to do with buffalo directly. But if they hadn't come, he might have felt too overwhelmed to pay attention.

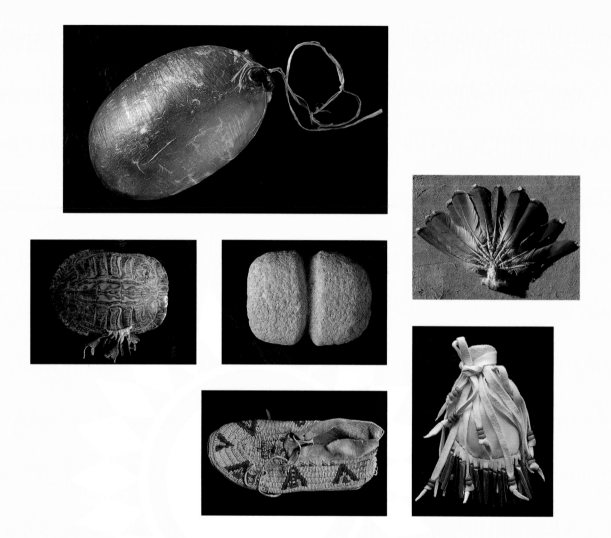

There was so much to learn about his culture. It seemed as if he discovered something new every day. For the first time, he realized that the tribe owned hundreds of artifacts. Ben showed Thunder Bear arrowheads that their ancestors had chipped from obsidian and other stone. He showed him how their people had carried water and other liquids in the bladder of a buffalo, which looked remarkably like a pale yellow balloon. Thunder Bear saw turtle shells, ornamented with the dewclaws of deer; ancient stone axe heads; and ceremonial fans made from the feathers of hawks, eagles, or turkeys. He saw beaded shoes and wristbands, like those his ancestors once traded from the Plains Indians. And there were thousands of potsherds—fragments of clay pots made by his ancestors hundreds of years ago. Most impressive of all was the medicine bag, made of soft deer hide, that contained sacred stones and other items with healing power.

It was forbidden to photograph the stones, or even to show them to outsiders. Thunder Bear had always wondered how he would find the courage to say that to an outsider, as his grandfather did. But now he no longer felt afraid.

The arrival of the buffalo also brought a spiritual and cultural renewal for Ben.

Sometimes he would take the afternoon off to make a drum. He hollowed out the trunk of an aspen tree, using a regular chisel, the sort that anyone might buy in a hardware store; but he hammered it with an elk antler.

Or he would sit quietly outside and make moccasins. He used a regular needle to sew the tiny buckskin moccasins, but instead of thread he used sinew, thin strips of animal tendon, just as his ancestors had done.

One afternoon, after a late-summer rain, Ben decided to hike in the nearby hilltops where his ancestors once lived. Centuries of blowing dust had buried their homes, hiding them so thoroughly that only an archaeologist could say exactly where they had once been. When Ben was a child, he used to play in the hills, but it had been a long time since he returned.

As he walked on the earth where his ancestors had walked, he found an ancient mano and two metates. People used these stone tools to grind corn and other foods.

Ben pulled the leaves of some of the edible plants growing nearby and sat quietly grinding them, pressing the mano against a metate. In the stillness that followed the rain, he could almost hear his ancestors speaking softly in Tewa. He could almost hear the sounds of children laughing as they herded the turkeys that provided meat when hunters came home empty-handed.

Ben and his friend Shannon talked about reviving ancient ceremonies that had disappeared from Nambe. They chose the eagle dance, a ritual that honors the eagle as a bridge between human beings and the sacred powers in the sky.

Ben and Shannon studied how people from other Pueblos swooped and soared as they danced in eagle costumes. Then, one stormy afternoon, the two men climbed high on a rocky outcropping overlooking Nambe Pueblo and practiced the centuries-old dance. Far below them, the buffalo grazed among the juniper trees. The new buffalo had become fully integrated into the herd. They were one big family now. Looking down at them, the men could feel the presence and power of the Buffalo Mother, silent, invisible, but there in the air all around them.

Eventually, the time came for Ben to kill one of the buffalo for meat. Like his ancestors, he prayed to the buffalo spirits that one animal would offer itself. He and Thunder Bear and Shannon honored the dead buffalo afterward by sprinkling sacred cornmeal on its head.

They gave meat to the villagers and saved the hooves to use in ceremonies. Nothing was thrown away.

Like their ancestors, they performed all the rituals of the hunt. Like their ancestors, they buried the jawbone of the animal so that its spirit would return. No outsider was present, so no outsider would ever know exactly where the jawbone lay, or what words were spoken on the dead animal's behalf.

Afterward, Shannon helped Ben by stretching the buffalo hide on a frame to keep it from crinkling and curling as it dried.

After the hide had lost all its moisture, Ben scraped it clean to get it ready for tanning, which softens the hide. He wanted to tan it the traditional way, using another part of the buffalo.

Over a little campfire, Ben heated the buffalo brains in a pot. "Eat the brains, Ben," someone joked. "You'll be smarter than a computer."

Ben laughed in his slow, quiet way. "No, man," he said. To himself, he thought how much he liked Pueblo Indian humor and the way it combines the old and the new.

He stirred the brew as it boiled. Then he smeared it across the buffalo hide.

"They say when you tan a skin, you should always use the brains of the animal you're tanning," he said. "Deer brains for deer. Elk for elk. Buffalo for buffalo."

Days later, after the hide had softened, Thunder Bear and Aaron watched while Ben drew pictures on the animal skin, just as his ancestors used to do.

First, he formed a circle. It represented the four sacred directions. Then he drew a buffalo bull. Then a kiva.

"What do these two ladder poles coming out of the kiva stand for?" he asked Thunder Bear.

Thunder Bear replied, "Summer People and Winter People."

The whole world was like a great circle, Thunder Bear thought. All of it fit together. The buffalo. The eagle dance. The Summer People and the Winter People. The present and the past. The oral history of Native Americans and the written history he learned in school. All of it was part of the mystery and power of life, of his life as a Pueblo Indian boy who would someday be the leader of the Winter People.

If he ever forgot what he knew today, the drawings on the buffalo skin would remind him.

Soon after that, Ben and the boys went out to see the buffalo again. Thunder Bear watched as each one munched a bite of wild grass, then moved a few feet and chomped another. With the animals that had come from Fort Wingate and the calves that had been born, there were almost thirty buffalo now. All of them were part of the buffalo nation. They were his brothers and sisters. And they were a link between the distant past and today, between his ancestors and him.

Thunder Bear knew now that he would spend the rest of his life learning about his traditions and his heritage. As Aaron and Tewa Breeze grew older, he would share what he knew with them. Someday, when it was time, he would become the new leader of the Winter People. And, like the people of Nambe Pueblo before him for hundreds of years, he would honor buffalo and the spirit of the buffalo all the days of his life.